"I'm a single mom and had Denise's help searching for scholarships for my son...In addition to his scholarships, he is managing all of his bills on his own. He won't even take free groceries from me! Then I decided to go to college! I have earned scholarships from 3 different organizations and my extra scholarships are building my emergency fund! Thank you for all you do and have done to help me and my son." ~ Joy

"I contacted Denise in my son's Sophomore year of high school. She guided me as to what was missing for college acceptance and scholarships. The next year he won an international scholarship to any college in the U.S. that covers everything including housing. I can sleep at night." ~ Cici

"Denise's strategies saved us more than $100k per child. They each came out of college with cash left over. We started while they were in middle school. This works!" ~Dennis

"My mom purchased Denise's services for me when my son was in middle school. He'll graduate from college with extra cash. I didn't know it was possible. I'm so grateful." ~Cindy

# How to Go to College Debt Free

## A Guide to College Acceptance and Scholarships

# How to Go to College Debt Free

## A Guide to College Acceptance and Scholarships

## How to Find Scholarships
### K through College

**Denise Thomas**

TEDx speaker and international best selling author

# How to Go to College Debt Free

# How to Find Scholarships
## K through College

# A Guide to College Acceptance and Scholarships

### by Denise Thomas

Published by Denise Thomas

Copyright © 2023 Denise Thomas

ISBN 13: 9798379104009

Produced in the United States of America

*Dedicated to Dennis, Brandi & Sean*

# CONTENTS

# FORWARD
## BY IMAN AGHAY

The first time I heard Denise speak about Debt Free College, I was intrigued. I wondered if it could really be possible. We hear a lot about the high cost of college and the student loan debt crisis, but it seems like there might be something we're missing.

Many of us assume that everyone in the U.S. has college debt because it's a common belief perpetuated by the media. However, the media doesn't tell us that young adults graduating with college debt take an average of 21 years to pay off their bachelor's degree. Even then, they might not be free of debt until their 40s, if they're lucky.

Then Denise said something that caught my attention: "Thirty percent of college students graduate debt-free every year. What are they doing that the rest aren't?"

Although there are many careers that require a college education, such as becoming a doctor or practicing law, getting through college can be incredibly expensive. All those professionals who graduate have to deal with a mountain of debt.

What's worse is that only 27% of people end up working in the field they studied for in college. Despite this, they still have to pay back their student loans, which they can't get rid of even if they go bankrupt.

While there are occasional government forgiveness programs, what if students could learn how to graduate from college debt-free in the first place?

On the other hand, those who graduate debt-free can enjoy the benefits of their college education and add financial freedom to fully explore the new adult world they've stepped into.

But achieving a debt-free college education doesn't just happen by chance. As Antoine de Saint-Exupéry said, "A goal without a plan is just a wish." That's where "How to Graduate Debt Free" comes in. It's part of the Cracking the Code to Free College strategy that Denise has shared with families for more than a decade.

It will require some work, but the benefits your children will enjoy on the other side will be worth it. Congratulations on taking the first step and investing your time in your child's future. You're giving your teen the best possible start.

Iman Aghay
Leaders Mentor
Founder and Director, Success Road Academy®

# NOTE FROM THE AUTHOR:
# JUST THE BEGINNING

By simply holding this book, your friends will think you've lost your mind, that you're putting too much pressure on your kid. The truth is just the opposite.

Getting ahead of the college admissions and scholarship game prevents stress and opens up the possibilities for your children. Ignore the nay-sayers. They don't have children and clients who graduated from college debt free with cash left over. Your goals and theirs are different. Remember, misery loves company, and with 70% of college students graduating with student loan debt, they have a lot of company. Do it differently. <u>Crack the Code to Free College.</u>

**"The earlier you start, the more opportunities you'll have."**
**~Denise Thomas**

This is *just the beginning*. I'm excited that you are getting started long before your peers. To get more in-depth and put these and other strategies into practice for your family, connect with Denise. Get the Cracking the Code to Free College online course for parents. Your children will thank you.

## To Your Success!
## Denise

SCAN QR CODE

www.GetADebtFreeDegree.com
Ask about the FREE Middle School ebook

Debt Free Degree Podcast:
https://www.getaheadoftheclass.com/podcast
Debt Free Degree TV:
https://www.youtube.com/c/DebtFreeDegreeTV

For downloads & free resources related to this book:
https://www.getaheadoftheclass.com/books

# CHAPTER 1

## EXPECTATIONS

Let me start by saying, if winning scholarships were easy, everyone would be getting free money. If it's too easy, it's a scam. I will talk about avoiding scholarship scams later in this book.

First let's set some expectations.

As you are looking for scholarship opportunities, you will undoubtedly find scholarships that are for older students or current college students. Do not toss them aside! If it looks like a possibility for the future then put it on your list for later.

The higher the dollar amount of the scholarship, the more involved the application will be. If a scholarship is for $10,000 it's likely there will be more than just an essay involved, with possibly letters of recommendation, good grades, or more.

There are scholarships for as young as kindergarten, no kidding, but there are hundreds of thousands of scholarships for high school seniors. Think of the number of scholarships available like a traditional bell curve or a mountain. From a young grade through college, grad school, and professional degrees, the highest number scholarship opportunities is in the middle of the curve, or top of the mountain, for high school seniors. The fewest scholarships available are for professional school or college seniors, and on the other side of the curve, for elementary students. Thus, don't get discouraged or overwhelmed. If you are looking for a high school freshmen, you may only find a few scholarships by the end of this week. But you will have the tools necessary to continue your search.

Scholarships whose application dates have not yet opened, may not show up in your search. If the scholarship application opens from August through November and you are looking in March, it may not show up in your search at all. What this means is that this book, this strategy, is not a "once and done." This is training you to know **where and how** to look for scholarships. Your journey is just beginning.

If you are a college student, still looking to increase your college fund, this is for you too! I'll give some additional tips just for current college students.

If you are *serious* about finding money for college, consider repeating this search at least once per month, looking for new scholarships that have come online, or applications that have opened. ... This system works!

### Notes

_____

_____

_____

# CHAPTER 2

# MONEY TERMINOLOGY

Although there is a reference chapter at the end of this book, Terms Your Need to Know, there can be a lot of confusion when it comes to college financial terminology. So we'll get that out of the way here.

(Financial Aid) **Award Letter**: A financial aid document sent to admitted students that outlines the terms of an awarded financial aid package.

**CSS Profile**: An additional financial application required by many private colleges in addition to the FAFSA. The CSS form was created by the College Board. However, each college can choose which of the 100 or so fields they want to use in their financial calculations. It is not free to file. For each college that requires the CSS profile you will have to pay a fee.

**Direct Student Loan** Direct Subsidized Loans and Direct Unsubsidized Loans are federal student loans offered by the

U.S. Department of Education to help eligible students cover the cost of higher education at a four-year college or university, community college, or trade, career, or technical school. (You might see Direct Subsidized Loans and Direct Unsubsidized Loans referred to as Stafford Loans or Direct Stafford Loans, but these aren't the official loan names.)

**Expected Family Contribution (EFC)**: This is the amount a student's family can be expected to contribute to one year of college expenses. Your EFC is based on your family's financial income and assets. It is then subtracted from the cost of attendance (COA) of attending each school you're admitted to. The resulting sum is considered your financial need, or the amount of financial aid you're eligible for.

**Free Application for Federal Student Aid (FAFSA)** The FAFSA is a financial aid form that must be filled out by all students seeking federal, and sometimes state, need based aid. Many colleges require the FAFSA. When filing the FAFSA you need to know which schools you want this financial information sent to. Your information will be sent to those colleges and universities for determining student need based aid. When a college accepts you they will send an acceptance letter along with an award letter listing any financial aid, scholarships, or work-study being offered, in addition to possibly offering a federal student loan, and a federal parent loan. Your initial FAFSA application has a maximum of 10 colleges you may list. If you need to add schools after you've submitted the FAFSA you must wait until the first set of colleges have received the information before making changes. Use the Make Corrections to a Processed FAFSA form or call the Federal Student Aid Information Center and submit your information to those additional schools no later than that school's last day of enrollment (or by mid-September of college freshman year).

Contact that school's admissions office or financial aid office to ask when their last day of enrollment is.

In your teen's college student portal on each of the college websites they have applied to, YOur teen will have to "accept" the aid that is being offered by checking the boxes. You don't have to accept all the financial aid you've been offered. Remember, scholarships and grants are 'gifts' that are not paid back. Federal loans are also listed under 'aid' but are not gifts. They do have to be paid back. Use caution and be sure you know exactly WHAT you are 'accepting'. It's not uncommon for student to click "accept" on student loans because the website might use abbreviations.

**Full-Ride Scholarship** A merit based scholarship which includes the entire cost of attendance. This includes Tuition, fee, room, and board (meal plan.) In may include additional items such as a stipend of books, the out of state tuition adder (if that applies to you), or a stipend toward a laptop.

**Grant** A grant is money given to a student for college that does not need to be repaid. Grants differ from scholarships in that they are awarded based on financial need, not merit.

**Need Based Aid** or Need based scholarships is award money based on the parent's income.

**Merit based scholarships-** are scholarships based mostly on the student's academic or artistic performance. It might be based on GPA, test scores, essays, or other academic or artistic prowess.

**Outside scholarships-** are monetary awards that are not given directly by your teens college or university. They are 'outside' the scope of the university. **They are also called Private Scholarships.**

**PSAT/NMSQT (Preliminary SAT/National Merit Scholarship Qualifying Test.):** The PSAT is standardized test and is the qualifying test for National Merit Scholarships.

**Parent PLUS Loan** Direct Parent PLUS Loans are unsubsidized loans made to parents of dependent undergraduate students. If a student's parents cannot get a parent PLUS loan, the student may be eligible to receive additional unsubsidized loans.

**Resident Assistant (RA)** This is a part-time on-campus job where the student works in their dormitory. Freshmen are not usually eligible to apply, and almost always, to apply your teen must have been living in the dormitory. Sometimes the criteria also includes a minimum GPA, and number of college credit hours completed prior to starting the position. The best part of being an RA is that in most colleges the RA's get their door room for free. This may be a private room. There can be additional monetary perks depending not he college, such as full or partial meal plan, and a small bi-weekly paycheck. It is not common but occasionally the college does not offer the free dorm room. In my opinion being an RA is too much work to not at leanest get $3000+ off of each semester cost.

**Scholarship** A scholarship is money given to students for college that doesn't need to be repaid. Scholarships are awarded based on academic, extracurricular, or athletic merit.

**Scholarship Displacement** If your teen qualifies for *need* based aid from the college or from the Federal Government, then additional scholarships will usually count against the student's need. What this means is that if the student is receiving the Federal Pell Grant, and/or Need Based award money from the college, then any additional scholarships will reduce the amount of the need based money.

Here's an analogy: When a school allows scholarship stacking, it's like having 2 apples, and you give me one more apple, I now have 3 apples. Yea!

HOWEVER IF YOU HAVE <u>NEED</u> BASED SCHOLARSHIPS The scenario plays out like this: I have 2 apples, and you give me one more apple; but they take one of my original 2 apples away, because my NEED isn't as great anymore, so I still have only 2 apples. SO WHAT WAS THE POINT OF LOOKING FOR THE OTHER APPLE?

At many SCHOOLS, when it comes to NEED BASED AID, Scholarship stacking doesn't always work out in the student's favor!

**Scholarship Stacking** is <u>very</u> important to you. You may or may not be aware of this awesome idea. Scholarship stacking is where your teen can have as many merit based or outside scholarships as your teen can win and they stack on top of the merit scholarships given by the college or university; Many times if the total winnings are in excess of the total bill for the college, your teen gets the extra cash in their bank account! HOWEVER, not all schools stack scholarships so you have to ask...

**Student Aid Report (SAR)**: This financial Student Aid Report, which includes the Expected Family Contribution, is sent to students after colleges receive the students' FAFSA.

When you receive it, immediately review it for accuracy. If you need to make changes, either because the information is incorrect or your financial situation has changed since you submitted your FAFSA form,  and have your FAFSA re-processed.

It will inform you if you are eligible for a federal grant, college loan, or work-study. It will also state if your application was

9

selected for verification. Each year some forms are selected for this process and your school confirms your information on the FAFSA is accurate. If your FAFSA is selected your school will tell you which documentation you are required to submit.

The SAR will also inform you if additional information or documentation is required to be eligible for federal aid. If no further information is needed, your SAR will also include your EFC (Expected Family Contribution)-see above.

**Subsidized Student Loan** Student loans accrue interest the moment the loan is distributed to the college on the student's behalf. With subsidized student loans the interest is paid by the federal government while the student is in college.

**Unsubsidized Student Loan** Student loans accrue interest the moment the loan is distributed to the college on the student's behalf. Although the student does not have to begin repayment until after they are out of college and after the grace period, the monthly interest is compounded throughout the student's time in college.

**Work-Study**: A federally (or sometimes state) funded program that gives a student a campus job in exchange for financial aid. The state or federal government subsidizes the university to pay for on-campus jobs for qualifying students.

# Notes

# CHAPTER 3

# MYTHS THAT KEEP OUR KIDS IN COLLEGE DEBT

While I was doing the research for my teens, I noticed that there were things that people believed to be true, and I heard them over and over again. Many these beliefs are the cause of our children ending up in college debt.

One of the first that I heard came from my very best friend.:

**Myth: "You're starting too early. Wait until junior year for that."**

However, what I found was that students who graduate college without debt started early. But what does that mean?

There are a lot of things that you can start early.

- Having the money conversation with your teens early in high school that says, here's where we are. This is what we're contributing towards your education, or not. When your teen is aware of the financial parameters early, he can set certain things in motion to increase his chances for college admissions and scholarships.

My parents never had that conversation with us. If the subject of college came up, all we heard was, "When you go to college…" not, "If you go to college…" With no one talking about the cost we assumed our parents were paying. It wasn't until the summer between my high school junior and senior year that the topic of paying for college came up. I'll never forget my mom relaxing on the couch as she said, "Oh, no. We're not paying for you to go to college. That's all on you."

What parents may not realize is that teenagers live in their own little world. They have a roof over their head and food on then table. They're good to go. They don't see the financial sacrifices you're making. They don't pay the bills you're paying.

When my mom said this, my little teenage world came crashing down. I had been working for two years and never saved a dime. I suddenly realized all of those Taco Bell and Burger King lunches I was buying on my work breaks added up to a semester college. I brought a sack lunch from home after that.

- Start working toward good grades and learning how to study. Your teen's grades from high school freshmen year count toward college admissions and scholarships.

- ACT and SAT test strategies and content. Waiting until junior year is not the strategy to take when you're hoping for scholarship money.

- Activities that win admissions and scholarships. Working on those activities that win admissions and scholarships is not necessarily a specific activity. It's knowing the criteria necessary to be in the running for the scholarships.

For example, my daughter is five years older than my son. When she was applying to one of the largest scholarships in the country, the application process begins with nine pages of checkboxes, of typical high school activities and leadership

14

roles. This part of the application is processed through a computer to find those applicants that will go through to the next round. My daughter was homeschooled and couldn't check enough boxes even though she had an impressive high school to college resume. Thus, her application didn't get past the computer.

My son, being five years younger, I now have the application. I know what boxes need to be checked. When you know what you don't know, early enough, you can make things happen for your children. When you don't begin this process until junior and senior year, you've left a lot of money on the table. For my son, we were able to craft or design his high school experience to be able to check those boxes, not to say, "It's on the list so you have to do it." That's not what I'm saying. Instead, show your teen the list of activities. "What looks like fun to you?" Choose what gets past the computer to get to the real application. If what your teen loves to do is not one of the checkboxes, that's fine. They should continue to do that thing that they love. But add a few of these other things so they are given the chance to show what they love. Get passed the first round of checkboxes to the real application, the one where they can actually fill out what they have accomplished. My son became a Coca Cola semifinalist. Knowing early what's important to the scholarship organization helps your kids.

- Applying for scholarships as early as kindergarten.

When I mention this, most people think that it's putting too much pressure on young children. But everything in the Cracking the Code to Free College strategy is just the opposite of pressure. The kindergarten scholarship is literally putting a coloring page in front of your child with a crayon. No stress.

## Myth: We make too much money to "get anything."

This is a common belief, but there are two sides to this myth.

One part is merit based scholarships while the other is need based aid from the colleges that your teen applies to.

We were not broke when my kids were winning and being awarded that nearly $200,000. We had grown the lawn care company to six figures within the first year. Before my daughter began applying for college and scholarships, my husband stepped out of the day-to-day business to focus on sales, and guaranteed his crew leader $100,000 per year. We were in the "we make too much to get anything" crowd.

When it comes to the financial offer by the college your teen applies to, there are private colleges that offer discounts based on your family income and assets. It's very possible that the $70,000 per year college could have a bottom line payment for your 6-figure family of less than $20,000 per year. Those discounts are largely due to the college having a large endowments. Your definition of "need" and the college's definition can be very different. However, most colleges that offer large need based discounts are not as generous with merit based scholarships.

Most merit based scholarships do not have a need (family income maximum) attached to it. Merit scholarships are based on what your teen does, their GPA, ACT or SAT scores, athletics, or artistic prowess.

Recently a parent asked how to find scholarships that are not need based. That's another assumption that everything out there is based on income or lack of income.

# Myth: You have to be a genius to win scholarships

I had been publicly speaking for years explaining the process but it wasn't until a parent came up to me afterward that I realized I had been leaving something pout of my keynote. She said, "Your kids must be geniuses because my kid applied to 40 scholarships and won none." It broke my heart to hear that. From that moment I always add to my presentations that, no, your kids do not have to be geniuses to win scholarships. Half of the scholarships my children won did not ask for GPA or test scores, a full $100,000 worth. Most private scholarships are just writing a short essay, an opinion on a topic.

# Myth: You have to attend a name recognized college to be successful in life

Let's stop right here. This is the most dangerous belief of all. If I can't convince you otherwise, stop reading, because nothing else will matter. Parents who are set on this belief are destined to have hundreds of thousands of dollars in student loan debt along with their teens. Why? Two reasons.

(1) Your teen is only allowed a very small amount of debt with out a co-signer. Tag-you're-it! You are the co-signer. Just when you thought you could ride off into the sunset and enjoy your later years, think again. That extra $200,000 plus in student loan debt you co-signed for is 100% your debt as much as it is your teen's. It affects your buying power.

(2) The most money in one bucket that your teen will have comes from the college he chooses to attend. When a family comes to me *after* their teen has committed to a college, and they tell me they have a $40,000 per year gap to fill between what the college has offered and what they can comfortably

afford, sorry, it's not possible to fill that gap. (I cover Choosing a College for the Cash in another book.)

The truth is, no one cares what college name is on your teen's diploma. No one! There is an extremely small number of employers that only hire from a specific college and chances are, even if that were your teen's goal, the likelihood of your teen being employed there is very slim Is it worth risking multiple 6-figures in debt?

Employers do not care what college your teen attends. They do care about what your teen accomplished while in college and they care about the grades your teen receives in college.

Many parents believe that their teen must attend a top 20 college. What does that mean? They're talking about the U.S. News and World Report College Rankings. This is a list that is published each fall. However, most people don't realize that the rankings have nothing to do with educational quality or student outcomes. There is no outside authority ranking colleges in this way. The U.S. News and World Report College Rankings get their information directly from the colleges. Colleges submit information such as average GPA of entering freshmen, average ACT or SAT score of entering freshmen, acceptance rate (percentage of applicants accepted, number of seats versus the number of applications they receive.) They are not ranking on whether or not the educational quality is good, bad, or great. They are not ranking on the income your teen will receive as a graduate of that college versus another college. The items mentioned are often manipulated to the college's advantage. Here is an example.:

Prior to the pandemic of Covid-19 only 10% of colleges in the U.S. were what is called "test optional." Test optional colleges allow the applicant to choose if they want to submit their ACT or SAT scores or not, for admissions decisions. It's "optional." It doesn't take a rocket scientist to conclude that students without great test scores are the ones *not* submitting scores. If mediocre or bad test scores are not submitted, colleges can't average those poor scores into the mix. This automatically increases their average entering freshman test score when they submit that information to U.S. News and World Report.

Another area easy to manipulate is the number of applications a college receives in any application timeframe. Colleges buy the names and address of students taking the PSAT, ACT, and SAT exams. They send postcards or letters to hundreds of thousands of students offering an application fee waiver to apply to their pricey college. They often mention the student's "high test score" when actually the college has no access to the student score. It's emotional manipulation at its finest.

What I have described is just a couple of methods colleges use to manipulate the numbers. This is considered legal and ethical. But every few years a college or two is caught outright cheating regarding the information they submit. When this happens they get a slap on the wrist and are banned from being on the list for a year or two.

If these expensive colleges were offering higher entry level salaries, they would be advertising it. Instead, they advertise smiling college students walking on oak tree lined paths. They are selling the experience. And we're buying it.

# What are some of the beliefs or myths you have surrounding high school and college?

_____

_____

_____

_____

_____

_____

_____

_____

_____

_____

_____

_____

_____

_____

_____

# Notes

# CHAPTER 4

## GETTING ORGANIZED

Before we get too far into organization remember that there are very few scholarships for under age 13. Due to there being so few, a quick google search for scholarships for under age 13 will cover it. One your child is in the 7th or 8th grades you can begin searching and organizing scholarships for high school freshmen and so on. At that point you'll be looking for the criteria necessary to apply, and preparing your teen for those requirements.

Start getting organized by setting up your scholarship organization system. There are many ways to stay organized and keep track of the scholarships that you would like your teen to apply to. I have used all three methods.

The three organizational methods are:
>Spreadsheet
>Folder on your computer
>Physical box and folders

### SPREADSHEET

The first method is a spreadsheet. I do like the spreadsheet. You can keep everything well organized and can re-organize it at anytime. You can sort the columns by due date, by scholarship dollar amount, or by any column.

Set up your spreadsheet with the following columns.:

The name of the scholarship

Website URL
Your Login (which is usually two columns. One for your email or username and the other for the password. Most scholarships will not require a login but some do.)

The scholarship dollar value amount $

Organization Contact information
(Optional: organization phone number, email - Necessary of you need to ask questions or clarify something.)

(Organization address - Necessary if some of the items needed have to be mailed.)

Criteria - You may need a separate column for each. You can add each column as you notice it's needed. Ot your can enter it all in one field on your spreadsheet.

Grade level

4-yr University

Minimum ACT or SAT score

GPA (Is almost always unweighted. Know the difference.)

Leadership

What they're looking for in an applicant or in the essay

Date the Scholarship opens

Date it closes (Deadline)

Date they contact the winner(s)- Your'll want this information because if the contact winner date has passed then you know your teen did not win, and can check the won or lost box in that row. You don't necessarily want to delete the scholarship row. If you have younger children, the scholarships may be available for them in later years. If the scholarship grade level includes higher grade levels, our teen can try again next year.

Time Zone-Great for not missing last minute deadlines.

Other Requirements: Transcript. Is an unofficial transcript ok at the application stage?

Essay-Number of words: Maximum or minimum

Letters of recommendation (how many?)

Does it require a resume?

Activities, awards, and honors? Is there a place to fill that on the application or do you provide a high school to college resume?

Family financial records?

Date your teen submitted the application.

Did your teen win or lose?

So if you get past May of the following year and you didn't hear

Scholarship Spreadsheet

| Name of Scholarship | URL Website | Login | $ Amount | Contact Info | Address | Criteria | Opens | Deadline | Transcript | Essay #Wds | Let. of Rec. | Resume | Finan. Info | Other | Date Submit | Date Award Announced | Won/ Lost |
|---|---|---|---|---|---|---|---|---|---|---|---|---|---|---|---|---|---|
| Burger King Scholars | https:// bkmclamorefoundation.org/who-we-are/programs/burger-king-scholars-program/ | | $1000-$50,000 | 507.931.8840 burgerkingscholars@scholarshipamerica.org | | Senior; 4-yr university; Minimum ACT 25/SAT 1220; Min GPA 3.3; Leadership & Work | October 15 | December 15 | n/a | n/a | n/a | activities awards honors | Y | Test scores | | May | |
| | | | | | | | | | | | | | | | | | |
| | | | | | | | | | | | | | | | | | |
| | | | | | | | | | | | | | | | | | |
| | | | | | | | | | | | | | | | | | |
| | | | | | | | | | | | | | | | | | |
| | | | | | | | | | | | | | | | | | |
| | | | | | | | | | | | | | | | | | |
| | | | | | | | | | | | | | | | | | |
| | | | | | | | | | | | | | | | | | |
| | | | | | | | | | | | | | | | | | |
| | | | | | | | | | | | | | | | | | |
| | | | | | | | | | | | | | | | | | |

then you're pretty darn sure you didn't win it.

For downloads & free resources related to this book: https://www.getaheadoftheclass.com/books

## DESKTOP FOLDERS

The method for keeping track of your scholarships is to use the folder on your desktop of your computer. In it I have 4 folders.:

"Scholarships Eligible to Apply To"
"Applied"
"Won"
"Lost"

Within the "Eligible" folder are separate folders for the different months of the year. (1 January, 2 February, etc) This represents the deadline date for each of the scholarships. I label numerically so it's easy to keep them in order.

The scholarship opportunities for each month are PDFs from the websites where I found them. Each PDF is labeled with the deadline to be certain I don't miss it.

Once your teen has applied for a scholarship, take a screenshot or PDF of the application that's been filled. And put it with any other information into the applied folder. Once you know if the student has won or lost the scholarship, move it to the appropriate folder.

So you begin to weed out January or February scholarships and you will put more into those folders as new ones you come upon with deadlines for the following year.

Scholarships are always available, so until your teen graduates from college or post grad school, continue looking.

## PHYSICAL BOX WITH FOLDERS

What is the physical folder method?

If you or your teen prefers to feel paper in your hands you'll need a box with file folders. I like colored folders to keep it interesting. Label folders for each month of the year.

I would print out the essay prompt and the deadlines for my teen. That way I could hand my teen the folder and say, "Here's what's coming up. You have 10 scholarships that are available for next month." They have the essay prompt and any info they need. My teen would write the essay on their computer and then copy and paste it to the scholarship website.

**Notes**

_____

_____

_____

_____

_____

_____

_____

_____

_____

_____

# CHAPTER 5

## USE YOUR TEEN'S UNIQUENESS

Let's start by making your scholarship search personal. Yes, there are hundreds of thousands of scholarship opportunities out there. But the ones your teen has a better than even chance of winning are the ones that are more personal to what your teen has to offer.

For example, there are scholarships for physical attributes such as being really short or really tall, for medical conditions such as legally blind, or for your religion, or ethnic heritage.

When your teen applies to scholarship opportunities, which are personal to them, their application will stand out among the crowd. In this chapter you will create your teen's personal keyword search list.

Set a timer, and brainstorm with your teen for 10 minutes. List everything your teen does, every activity in and out of school, school clubs, church, religious affiliation, family ethnicity, heritage, volunteer community service, employment, entrepreneurship skills, personal characteristics, such as left handed, what might be their potential college major? Where do the teens parents work? There is a scholarship for red hair. There's a duck calling contest, a fishing scholarship, amateur ham radio scholarships. Does your teen advocate for socially conscious or political things? Many offer scholarships, you get the picture.

Parents, call the HR department of your employment and ask if they offer college scholarships for the children of employees. You'd be surprised how many parents are not aware of this.

At this point, you've only spent about 10 minutes. Next, you'll discover how to use the keywords to find a list of potential scholarship applications.

If you're having trouble coming up with a list of keywords check the list on the next page for additional ideas *after* you and your teen have already given this your best shot. I don't want you to miss something because you got distracted with a list.

A large part of graduating college debt free is choosing the right college. The largest scholarship will come from the college or university itself as an entering freshman scholarship. There are a lot of factors involved in choosing a college with over 3000 4-year colleges and universities in the U.S. I discuss Choosing a College for the Cash in a later book.

# Here are some ideas for personal attribute keywords:

Learning Disabilities
Physical Disabilities
Medical conditions
Diabetes
Military affiliation
Adopted/Foster child/orphan Cancer patient/Survivor or child of Child of single parent
Overcoming Adversity
Race
Credit union member
Twins/Triplets Domestic
abuse victim
Gender
Duck calling contest
Environmental activism
Honors organization
Academic Major
Farmer
First in family college student (first generation)
Anti-bullying
Pet/Animal Care
Bilingual
Vegetarian/Vegan
Affected by 9/11 attacks
Homeless / Formerly homeless
LGBTQ, Parent LGBTQ or LGBTQ ally
Migrant worker/Child of migrant worker
Multiple sibling (or parent of)
Refugee/Immigrant
Returning/Continuing Student
Single parent
Undocumented/TPS/DACA
Social Action

Transplant candidate/Recipient
Student with Dependent Children
Transfer students
Study Abroad
Student organizations and social organizations (criteria may
include membership, geographic location, specific college/
university) but many. organizations do not require membership.:
4-H
American Legion
American Library Association
American Medical Women's Association American Quarter
Horse Association American Society of Civil Engineers Boy
Scouts
Civil Air Patrol
Daughters of the American Revolution Distributive Education
Clubs of America (DECA) Elks National Foundation
Future Farmers of America
Future business leaders of America
Girl Scouts
International Student Organization
Junior Achievement
Key Club
Beta Club
SkillsUSA
Boys Club/Girls Club
Youth for Christ

# Notes

# CHAPTER 6

# THE KEYWORD SEARCH

Keywords are just an idea of what a scholarship might be given for. Your list may have 10 or it may have 30 items. The more the merrier and the more possible opportunities.

You should also have a spreadsheet created on your computer to keep t4rack of the scholarships you find.

Decide how long you want to be at your computer. And let's get started.

You want to start your search as follows. Type in the words "scholarships for" and then *one* of your keywords and hit enter.

You can use the word "award" instead of scholarships, but usually the word scholarship shows what you're looking for. If you don't see anything on the first page of your search, you may go to page two. But if there is one, you'll likely find it on page one of your search if it's on the internet at all.

When you find scholarships that fit the keyword, you can either copy the website URL now and paste it into your spreadsheet or look through the scholarship information for eligibility *criteria* to know if or when your teen–may qualify for it. And then paste the URL into the spreadsheet.

You'll get used to scanning the scholarship website quickly to know if your qualifications match or not. Make it into a game for yourself and try not to spend more than 30 seconds deciding if it's a good fit.

If your teen will never qualify, then delete or don't add it to your scholarship spreadsheet. If they'll qualify in the future, perhaps as a college sophomore, add that information into the criteria for later.

As you're doing your search, you'll notice databases of scholarships. Sometimes you can get directly to the scholarship website. Other times they want you to join their database. It's okay to look. But please don't sign up for anything just yet. I'll show you how to use them properly later. If you can get in a database website without joining, click on the scholarship link. Usually you can get the name of the scholarship or the sponsor, and then do a separate search for that specific scholarship website. You'll quickly begin to recognize the names of the scholarship databases. It's important to note that some scholarship websites are not maintained throughout the year.

For example, if you search for scholarships for red hair, there is one it's called scholarship red. And it's been around since 2009. But the website page isn't maintained after they give the award in May of each year. Since the application isn't open, you won't find out much about it. This is one that you'll add it to your scholarship spreadsheet and look for it every couple of months waiting for it to open. Most scholarship applications are open at least two months prior to the deadline.

Now let me reiterate this. This is not, "find every scholarship this second." This is a process. Today, find at least one scholarship, preferably two or three, even if it's using only one of your keywords. You don't want to go through all your keywords in one sitting. You do have a life and responsibilities and this takes time.

## Notes

_____

_____

_____

_____

_____

_____

_____

_____

_____

_____

_____

_____

_____

# Notes

# CHAPTER 7

## YOUR TOWN - FINDING LOCAL MONEY

The first list is personal. Now we are adding external keywords. You're going to add to the keyword list and do another search. Take out the keyword list you started and add the following. :

The name of your city or town

Your county

Your state

Where does your family bank?

Where do they eat out?

Where do you shop?

Brainstorm a list for another 10 to 20 minutes.

If you can't think of much, I suggest the parent and teen take a drive around town together. Whoever's in the passenger seat, take notes and write the names of every business you pass, Taco Bell, Burger King, Walmart, they all offer scholarships! This does not have to be a business or organization you've ever been to. No one in our family was ever associated with the Elks club. Yet, both of my teens won scholarships from them. Write down every business, or organization, or take a video as you drive by and write them down later.

For keywords you added today, you're going to search the keywords as follows. "Name of business" scholarship. Some businesses will offer scholarships to their employees, others for local community or both. Some may be for students nationwide, such as Taco Bell, Burger King, and Walmart. For the keywords of where you live, search name of state or town and the word "scholarship", or name of town and the words "Community Foundation Scholarship." You can also use your state for that search.

List what you find in your spreadsheet. Go through the scholarship information for the criteria. If your teen does not qualify today, will they qualify in the future? Or is there something they can do later that will qualify them, such as a community service project? Find at least one scholarship your teen qualifies for based on your local keyword search.

# Notes

# CHAPTER 8

# THE COLLEGE STUDENT'S "LOCAL" SCHOLARSHIP SEARCH

If your teen is in or accepted to college there is another potential scholarship search they can do before reporting to general or database searches.

Look for the online catalog for the college or university. If your teen attends a large state university the catalog is likely to be found online. Look for the section for Financial Aid and Scholarships department. Check if they have scholarships listed by "college" or "department." Many companies that recruit from those colleges will offer scholarships, such as Dow Chemical offering upper class men scholarships to chemistry majors. There are also scholarships named after alumni from the college. If you find a page or two with those scholarships listed, look through them for qualifications such as class, GPA, and college major. If your teen qualifies for any, take a screenshot and send it to them.

Then at the start of every semester of college, your teen should go to the Department of their college major and to the Office of Financial Aid to ask if there are any scholarships for current students. There are almost always scholarships available for upperclassmen, both from the college and from generous alumni. Many times the student manning the desk has no idea what you are talking about. This is why it's a good idea to have that screen shot image of the list of scholarships available. Bump it up the chain of command until your teen finds someone who knows where the applicant for then scholarship is. But don't wait too long. Most of the time, the deadlines are in the first week or two of starting classes. Again, do this every semester. As the saying goes, the opera ain't over till the fat lady sings. And in this context, it means don't stop looking for scholarships until college graduation. Continue using every technique in this series until there are no more options. I talk more about what scholarship committees look for in my Cracking the Code of Free College online course.

# Notes

# CHAPTER 9

## LEARNING FROM PAST WINNERS

Next we'll search the keywords with names of other students in your area. You are looking for the newspaper articles which may list the names of the scholarships that were awarded to these students. This is more easily found in the late spring or early summer when announcements are made. Here are some ways of finding this information.

Look in the community news section of your local newspaper. It can be online or in print, preferably during the spring and early summer months. For an internet search, use the name of your town newspaper and graduating senior or graduate. You might see a photo of the student and a quick rundown of the scholarships they were awarded.

You can also attend the local high school senior awards nights and take notes, or pick up an award night program, if the student awards are listed.

Do an internet search for your local high school and add the keyword valedictorian or salutatorian, or National Merit semifinalist or National Merit finalist.

After finding the names of these students do another search. Search the name of the student and the word scholarships after their name. See if there's an article that leads you to the name of the scholarships some of these students have won. If you find them, copy and paste the names of the scholarships to your spreadsheet. Later, when you have time, do a search for those scholarships. Check the criteria and add the information to your spreadsheet if your student qualifies.

To be honest, this can be one of the most difficult areas of searching depending on the time of year. So if you find yourself spending too much time, don't be discouraged. What you seek may not be easily found today. Also, someone who lives in a large metropolis such as Dallas, Texas will have a lot more of these to sift through than someone from a small town. Your results may vary. That's okay. Your challenge today is to find one scholarship in your area that was not awarded directly by a college. I'm not asking for more than one because it can be difficult depending on the time of year. Remember, searching can lead to a rabbit hole. So set a timer. Spend 10 to 20 minutes searching for this information. You have a life. Finding scholarships can feel like an easter egg hunt and you can lose track of time.

# Notes

# CHAPTER 10

# YOUR SCHOOLS

When we hear people talk about local scholarships this is what is generally meant by it. These are opportunities where your local high school counselor should have a list. It's not always that easy.

For this next search, go to the websites of every local high school, both public and private in your area. Also, go to the local school board website. What you're looking for is a list of local and national scholarships. They may also have links to several scholarship databases. Remember, do not register for these website databases just yet, we'll discuss how to go about navigating national databases in another chapter. If the school lists this information it may be under guidance, or resources for seniors or parents. If they list any scholarship that you do not already have on your spreadsheet, copy and paste it there. Remember, sometimes these resources can be buried, sometimes you have to call the high school counselor and ask, and sometimes the school or the district is no help whatsoever.

Again, set a timer so you're not spending all day. If you live in a small rural community. You can also check the websites for high schools in nearby larger towns or cities. Remember to look at the scholarship website for the criteria.

If you don't find a scholarship list on the school or the district website, call the school guidance counselor office, they may have a list that they can email to you. It is possible that if your teen is not a student at that school, they may not take the call. But it's also possible you could get a list.

And one last thing to do today, go to your personal Facebook or social media profile and post this question. "What scholarships did your teens apply for?" You never know what a friend or relative will respond with.

**"Pay no attention to the man behind the curtain."**

**~ The Wizard**

Pay no attention to the nay sayers telling you that since their kids didn't win scholarships that your teen shouldn't bother. Misery loves company. In my experience, those who don't win, either applied to the wrong scholarships or didn't know how to win them. There is a strategy that wins. No geniuses required.

# Notes

# Notes

# CHAPTER 11

## AVOIDING SCHOLARSHIP SCAMS

This is something you'll find more often when you begin searching through national databases, which I'll introduce to you soon.

It's true, there are a ton of scholarship opportunities out there. 1.8 million scholarships for a total of 23 billion dollars is given away every year. But the easy thing to do is to apply to those that require very little effort.

Remember, if it's too good to be true, it probably is.

1       If all they're asking for is name and email address it's probably just a random drawing or sweepstakes. The only reason an organization would do this is to get your email address or to sell it. Yes, they are probably giving away $1,000 every month but it may take years to stop getting solicitation emails. It's not always easy to click unsubscribe.

Legitimate competitions require something, anything, that takes a little work. It could be a video, an essay, decent grades, letter of recommendation, or a list of activities. Just a short 200 word essay is better than nothing. But you'll want to read the fine print on those that are one sentence or just your email. It may cause more trouble than good, so be a little wary.

2      Never pay money to submit a scholarship application. If the company needs $7 to process it, they don't have enough money to be giving it away.

3      Avoid identity theft. Never give the social security number. I say never. But that's not 100% the case.

A large scholarship will usually require an IRS tax form to be filed. Do not give the Social Security Number one rate phone. The organization should already have your address when you submitted the application, so they should not ask for that either. If it's legit, they will call or send an email to announce that you've won. Then they will followup with a letter containing the forms you need to fill out and return to them.

Don't get discouraged when there's work involved. If the scholarship takes a lot of work, research paper, letters of recommendation and interview, etc. Rejoice. It will take a few hours. But put together it severely reduces the pool of applicants ,especially if it's a local or state scholarship, rather than a national one.

# Notes

# CHAPTER 12

# THE NO ESSAY SCHOLARSHIP

What about scholarships without essays? What if your teen is totally terrible at writing essays? Undoubtedly, the most time consuming part of filling out a scholarship application is writing the essay. So are the no essay scholarships legitimate? Well, think about it, there are more than a million scholarships offered every year. And the vast majority require something more than just a name and email address.

As I mentioned earlier in avoiding scholarship scams, you're taking a chance when applying to these types of offers. The odds of winning these scholarship sweepstakes, or random drawings are slim, extraordinarily slim. Yes, if you've done your research on it, it can be legitimate, meaning someone is going to win that $1,000. If your teen has no other scholarships to apply to at the time, then applying is a personal choice. I advise caution because your email may be spammed. Maybe use a different email only for this type of application. At the very least, try to go for the easy ones that have small essay requirements such as 100 to 300 words, or maybe a video requirement ,or something, anything more than just the name and email. That's not too difficult and it still might reduce the number of applicants, although not greatly.

# Notes

# CHAPTER 13

# NAVIGATING NATIONAL DATABASES - THE RIGHT WAY

Now let's talk about national databases. Every month more scholarships open applications. There are many who don't like using scholarship databases. They say it's too hard to win national scholarships. Only apply to local scholarships. While I agree there will be less competition with local and state scholarships, despite what you may have heard, these sites can be extraordinarily valuable if you know how to use them. My daughter's very first scholarship was a national one of $10,000 from a scholarship we would never have known about, had we not been searching this national database.

When registering for these national databases, they will send dozens of emails every day. It will overwhelm your personal email inbox. First your teen will create two new email addresses. While not technically required, I highly recommend one separate email for to register for these databases. This email can be anything. It will only be used to log into the database to find scholarships and nothing else. No-one will ever see this. I call this a "junk" email.

The second new email is used for applying for scholarships and college applications. Your teen will need a professional email with their name in it. They will need contact information including a professional email address for both scholarships and college applications. For example, john doe a@gmail.com or john dot doe dot A at gmail dot com, or john dot a@gmail.com. If the professional email name your teen wants isn't available, then you can add numbers or add Mr or miss in front of it.

This professional email will be used in resumes, college applications, employment applications, and these scholarship applications, so make it count. If they already have a professional email with their name, is it checked often? Is it overwhelmed with junk. If it's full of junk, then they either need to clean up the clutter or get a new email. This is so they will not miss anything important that comes while submitting college and scholarship applications. Most correspondence is through email today.

Be sure to keep the email and the password where you'll find it so that you can get to the emails in the inbox when needed. Refer to this link for an easy tutorial that shows you exactly how to get a free Gmail email account. There is no limit to how many gmail emails you can have. https://support.google.com/mail/answer/56256?hl=en

Next, your teen should register for a Fastweb scholarship database account using the "junk" scholarship search gmail account they have just created. https://www.fastweb.com/

Keep the registration log in handy. Your teen should fill in as much information as possible. The database will ask questions such as student's age or grade level, it may ask for their interest or to check boxes of things such as clubs that they've been in, or ACT and SAT test scores. When completed they'll do their first search.

Most of the time when you log into your database account with Fastweb, there will be a few pages of offers that your teen possibly has no interest in, such as college loans, online colleges, or Army National Guard. At the *top right corner* of those pages, it gives you the option to "skip this offer." You may have one or several, so just keep skipping to get to the scholarships.

Once you get to the actual scholarships page, notice the number of new scholarships. This is the number of new scholarships that have opened since the last time you logged in. If you loved in yesterday it may have a zero since nothing new has opened since then.

You'll also see the total dollar amount of the scholarships currently available. This is the potential value of the matches of scholarships that are available to your teen right now. They also list the total number of scholarships that are available to your teen.

The first scholarships listed as "top scholarships" I will generally ignore because they will also be in the full list. I'd rather order them by deadline.

You'll also see a scrolling list of additional scholarship opportunities. However, most of the3se are not really scholarships. Most of these are going to be sweepstakes, or random drawings. Go down a little further to actually see the matches.

This is likely to me multiple pages. Also in this list, you'll see scholarships that are listed as "featured". Featured are again likely to be random drawings or sweepstakes.

On the right side of each scholarship listed you also have the option to delete it, or mark it as interested, or not interested. So you can choose whether or not to look through them find out what they really are. For me, I generally mark them as not interested. They will be placed in the Tab "Not Interested."

Your scholarship matches can be ordered or organized in three different ways. You can organize them by name by clicking on the word name at the top of the list.

You can organize them by "amount of the award" by clicking on "award." It will go from the largest amount to the smallest.

You can organize them by "deadline." I prefer to organize by deadline, since that allows me to not miss any deadlines.

Sometimes you'll notice a scholarships that is near the top but it's not in the order by deadline. Why? Because it's a "featured" scholarship. Featured means it's being paid for by the sponsor to be placed in a prominent location where someone will see it.

As with the other scholarships you have found thus far, once you click on a scholarship you can probably know in under 30 seconds if your teen will qualify to apply for it.

If I think this is a scholarship that my teen would want to apply to, I would take the URL from the website, copy it, and then place it in the scholarship spreadsheet

A few tips:

1       Most of the scholarships today will require your teen to fill in an online application including the essay. It's always best to write the essay in a document and then copy and paste it into the field when they're ready.

2       Always check out the rest of the website. You may find information about a previous winner. It's always good to check that out. Sometimes they'll actually give you the entire essay that the last year's winner submitted.

3    What about that new Gmail email inbox? Ignore it. The new email account will be inundated with lists of scholarships several times each day. The databases are paid to show you a list of scholarships that your teen may not even have an interest in. So ignore the new Gmail inbox.

**Notes**

_____

_____

_____

_____

_____

_____

_____

_____

_____

_____

_____

_____

_____

# CHAPTER 14

## WHAT'S NEXT?

Applying for private scholarships is very enticing. Most people think they will win enough to cover their college costs. Is it possible? Yes. But it's not probable without the scholarship from the college your teen applies to. Look for the book, Choosing a College for the Cash, or join Cracking the Code to Free College to get the full strategy from early high school to college and create the winning college and scholarship package.

Finding scholarships is just the beginning. Winning takes strategy. Knowing what the scholarship committees are looking for and presenting your teen's application as the winner. A step int he right direction is the 12 Scholarship Secrets checklist. Go to the GetAheadOfTheClass.com website to request a copy.

Apply to as many scholarships as possible. With hundreds of thousands of scholarships available just for high school seniors there is probably several scholarships each week your senior can apply for. Doing everything right, it's still a numbers game. Don't stop looking for scholarships.

# TERMS YOUR NEED TO KNOW

The following terms are briefly defined so that you can have an understanding of the terms and acronyms you'll begin hearing regularly in the high school to college journey. Links to more details can be found at www.getaheadoftheclass.com/blog/terms-you-need-to-know

**ACT**: A standardized test used for national college admissions. All 4-year colleges and universities in the US accept ACT scores.

**Associate's Degree**: This is a 2-year degree typically offered by junior or community colleges, and sometimes at 4-year colleges and technical schools.

**AP Classes/Tests** (Advanced Placement Classes/Tests): The AP program offers standardized courses that give students the ability to earn college credit while in high school. Credit is accepted by participating colleges for students who score high enough on AP tests.

**Award Letter**: A financial aid document sent to admitted students that outlines the terms of an awarded financial aid package.

**Bachelor's Degree**: This is a 4-year degree typically offered by 4-year colleges and universities.

**Class Rank**: Class rank measures how your grade point average (GPA) stacks up against your peers.

**Common Application (Common App)**: A standard, free application form used to apply to over 450 American colleges and universities.

**Concentration (Major)**: An area of concentration in a particular field of study. Students typically declare their major by the end of their sophomore year of college.

**CSS Profile**: An additional financial application is required by some colleges in addition to the FAFSA.

**Deferred Admission**: When a student applies to a top choice college as "Early Decision", the college can reply in one of 3 ways: accepted, rejected, or deferred. Deferred means your application will be reconsidered along with other regular applications. The college may have some questions about whether you and the college are a good fit. Call the admissions office to ask why you were deferred. Remain professional when you call. Reiterate your strong interest in attending that college or university, and ask if you can provide them with additional information or work on any areas to improve your likelihood of being admitted. Ask how many deferred candidates are ultimately accepted. This will help you be realistic about how likely your efforts will produce an acceptance at that college.

Once you find out your application was deferred, work on ways of improving yourself as a candidate. If grades are the issue, write a letter to let the college know if you've scored good grades since you submitted your application. If the concerns are more general, let them know about any organizations you've joined or honors you've received since you sent in your application. You may want to submit an additional letter of recommendation from a respected adult who can speak highly of you.

**Early Action (EA)**: Under this admission program, a student can apply early to more than one college but is not bound to attend if accepted.

**Early Decision (ED)**: Under this admission program, a student can apply early to only one choice college as Early Decision and must attend this college if accepted. While waiting on a response the student can apply Early Action or Regular Decision to additional colleges.

**Expected Family Contribution (EFC)**: This is the amount a student's family can be expected to contribute to one year of college expenses. Your EFC is based on your family's financial income and assets. It is then subtracted from the cost of attendance (COA) of attending each school you're admitted to. The resulting sum is considered your financial need, or the amount of financial aid you're eligible for.

**Free Application for Federal Student Aid (FAFSA)**: The FAFSA is a financial aid form that must be filled out by all students seeking federal, and sometimes state, need based aid. Most colleges require the FAFSA. When filing the FAFSA you need to know which schools you want financial information sent to. Your information will be sent to those colleges and universities for determining student aid. When a college accepts you they will send an acceptance letter along with an award letter listing any financial aid, scholarships, or work-study being offered. If you need to add a school after you've submitted the FAFSA you'll have to make that change on your Make Corrections to a Processed FAFSA form or call the Federal Student Aid Information Center and submit your information to that school by that school's last day of enrollment (or by mid-September of college freshman year). Contact that school's admissions office or financial aid office to find out when their last day of enrollment is.

You don't have to accept all the financial aid you've been offered. Remember, scholarships and grants are 'gifts' that are not paid back. Federal loans are also listed under 'aid' but are not gifts. They do have to be paid back. Use caution and be sure you know exactly WHAT you are 'accepting'.

**Gap Year**: A gap year refers to a student taking a year after he graduates high school before he continues his education in college. Some students take a gap year to travel, for an internship, community service, work, or college prep or to better prepare their application to be accepted to the school of their choice.

Not all colleges will defer your scholarships for one year. So check with your intended college before taking a gap year. Those that do, will usually require your deposit before May 1 to ensure your seat.

**Grade Point Average (GPA)**: A GPA is a calculated average of the letter grades a student earns throughout high school. GPA indicates overall academic performance.

**Grant**: A grant is money given to a student for college that does not need to be repaid. Grants differ from scholarships in that they are awarded based on financial need, not merit.

**Humanities**: Humanities courses are courses that focus on human culture and development, including art, religion, music, literature, and foreign languages.

**Independent Study**: This form of study allows students to design coursework under the instruction of a faculty member.

**Legacy**: A legacy is a college applicant whose parents or grandparents graduated from the prospective school.

**Liberal Arts**: A liberal arts education exposes students to a broad course of study, including humanities, social sciences, mathematics, and natural sciences.

**Major (Concentration)**: An area of concentration in a particular field of study. Students typically declare their major by the end of their sophomore year of college although some colleges expect a student to choose a major field of study sooner.

**Minor**: A minor is a secondary field of study, typically different from one's major.

**Need-Based Financial Aid**: Need-based financial aid is financial aid based on a student's family's inability to pay full tuition.

**Open Admission**: An admissions type, usually found at community colleges or online schools, that admits all students who hold a high school diploma or GED.

**PSAT/NMSQT (Preliminary SAT/National Merit Scholarship Qualifying Test.)**: The PSAT is standardized test and is the qualifying test for National Merit Scholarships.

**Registrar**: College registrars manage student records, schedule classes, prepare transcripts, and collect college tuition and fees.

**Residential Life**: The college department that manages dorms and on-campus housing.

**Rolling Admissions**: An admissions type that allows students to apply at any time during the admission period, usually on a first-come, first-serve basis.

**SAT (Scholastic Assessment Test)**: The SAT reasoning test is the most widely-used standardized test for college admissions.

**Scholarship**: A scholarship is money given to students for college that doesn't need to be repaid. Scholarships are awarded based on academic, extracurricular, or athletic merit.

**Standardized Tests**: These tests evaluate academic skills and provide academic performance reports to educational professionals like teachers, professors, and admissions officers.

**Student Aid Report (SAR)**: This financial Student Aid Report, which includes the Expected Family Contribution, is sent to students after colleges receive the students' FAFSA.

When you receive it, immediately review it for accuracy. If you need to make changes, either because the information is incorrect or your financial situation has changed since you submitted your FAFSA form,  and have your FAFSA re-processed.

It will inform you if you are eligible for a federal grant, college loan, or work-study. It will also state if your application was selected for verification. Each year some forms are selected for this process and your school confirms your information on the FAFSA is accurate. If your FAFSA is selected your school will tell you which documentation you are required to submit.

The SAR will also inform you if additional information or documentation is required to be eligible for federal aid. If no further information is needed, your SAR will also include your EFC (Expected Family Contribution)-see above.

**Super score**: This is the average of the highest individual section scores of several ACT exam dates or the sum of your highest section scores across different SAT test dates. If the super score or super composite is used, this increases the probability of higher scholarships based on test score, and possibly skipping out of freshman year introductory courses in English and Math.

**Transcript**: The official record of a student's academic process, in high school or college.

**Undergraduate**: A college student working toward an undergraduate associate's or bachelor's degree.

**Valedictorian**: Valedictorian is a title given to a student at a high school graduation. Usually, this title is given to the highest-ranked student in the graduating class.

**Wait List**: A list of applicants who might be accepted once admitted students decided whether to accept or reject a school's offer.

**Work-Study**: A federally (or sometimes state) funded program that gives a student a campus job in exchange for financial aid. The state or federal government subsidizes the university to pay for on-campus jobs for qualifying students.

# ABOUT THE AUTHOR

Denise Thomas is a native of New Orleans, Louisiana, and attended college on the Pell Grant for low income families. While in college she worked 3 jobs and still had to 'lift' food from the college cafeteria so she could eat on the weekends. She didn't want her children to struggle as she had.

Denise homeschooled her two children from Pre-k through high school. After a devastating bankruptcy and liquidation, Denise had to create a way for her children to pay for college and gain acceptance as homeschooled students. Thousands of hours of research resulted in Denise's proprietary repeatable Cracking the Code to Free College strategy and her teens attended their first-choice college on 17 scholarships exceeding $199,000, walking out of college with cash in hand. They got paid to go to college!

Denise is an advocate for the U.S. military since, at age 10, watching her dad attain his degree from Tulane University on the G.I. bill and her company offers special opportunities for our military veteran and active duty families. Her company, Get Ahead of the Class, LLC also supports Spikes's K-9 Fund, a non profit that supplies protective gear for our furry friends in uniform.

Denise is a TEDx speaker, conference keynote speaker, international best-selling author, and coach to parents of college-bound teens. Denise inspires, educates, and equips parents to take an active role in supporting their children to live a life of financial freedom. Using her Cracking the Code to Free College strategy, her mission is to 'flip' the student debt statistic in the U.S.

Denise's podcast, Debt Free Degree, ranks in 4 countries; she is the host of Debt Free Degree TV YouTube channel, and College Prep for Success online summit for parents of middle school, high school, and college age children.

Denise says, "You can keep your money. Send your kids to college on other people's cash!" and "College doesn't have to be a debt sentence."

For downloads & free resources related to this book:
https://www.getaheadoftheclass.com/books

Connect with the author:

More books: https://amzn.to/41f9FXg
Website: https://GetAheadOfTheClass.com
Blog: https://www.getaheadoftheclass.com/blog
TEDx Talk: College Myths that Cost You Money https://www.getaheadoftheclass.com/media
Podcast: https://www.getaheadoftheclass.com/podcast